SMART BRAIN RIGHT BRAIN

Basic Geometry

Om KIDZ
An imprint of Om Books International

Om Kidz | Om Books International

Reprinted in 2023

Corporate & Editorial Office
A-12, Sector 64, Noida 201 301
Uttar Pradesh, India
Phone: +91 120 477 4100
Email: editorial@ombooks.com
Website: www.ombooksinternational.com

Sales Office
107, Ansari Road, Darya Ganj
New Delhi 110 002, India
Phone: +91 11 4000 9000
Email: sales@ombooks.com

Author: Shweta Sinha
Editor: Kirti Pathak
Art & Design: Anshuman Pandey, Gaurav Bhandari, Harish Arya

ISBN: 978-93-5276-857-8

Printed in India

10 9 8 7 6 5 4 3 2

CONTENTS

1. Shapes, Shapes, Shapes 4
2. Plane Shapes 6
3. Activity: Terrific Tangrams 14
4. Solid Shapes 18
5. Let's Get Active 28

Glossary 32

Answers 32

1. Shapes, Shapes, Shapes

Shapes are everywhere. Wherever you are, you can find shapes around you. How many circles, rectangles and triangles can you spot?

A **circle** is shaped like the letter 'O'. A circle is like a ball. It goes round and round with no start and no end.

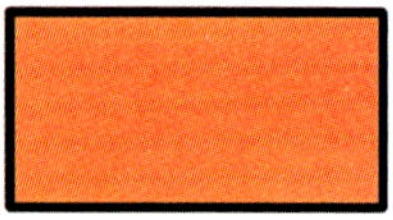

A **rectangle** has four sides. Opposite sides of a rectangle are of the same size.

A **square** is a special rectangle where all sides are the same size.

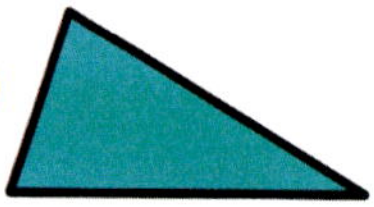

A **triangle** has three sides. The sides may or may not be of the same size.

An **ellipse** is like a circle that has been stretched. An ellipse is more wide than it is high.

DID YOU KNOW?

A pentagon is a shape with five sides, while a hexagon has six sides.

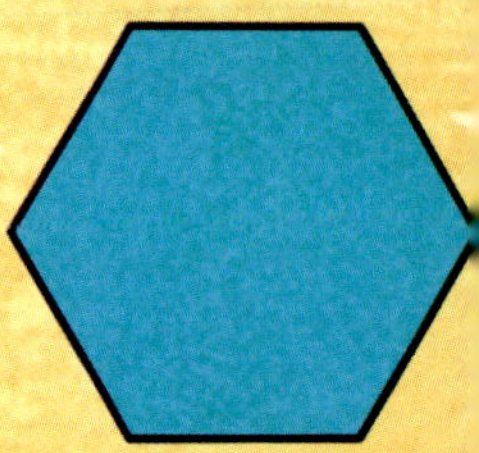

Bianca's lunchbox is filled with all her favourite things. Can you identify the shapes in it?

2. Plane Shapes

Plane shapes or 2-D shapes are flat shapes that you can draw on paper. 2-D stands for 2-dimensional. A 2-D shape has two dimensions - length and breadth. The sides of a 2-D shape can be straight or curved lines. Two dimensional shapes do not have thickness.

DID YOU KNOW? A sheet of paper is a 2-D object.

What is a dimension?

A straight line is one-dimensional. When you have one dimension, you can only go in one direction. You can only measure the length of a line. It has no breadth and no thickness.

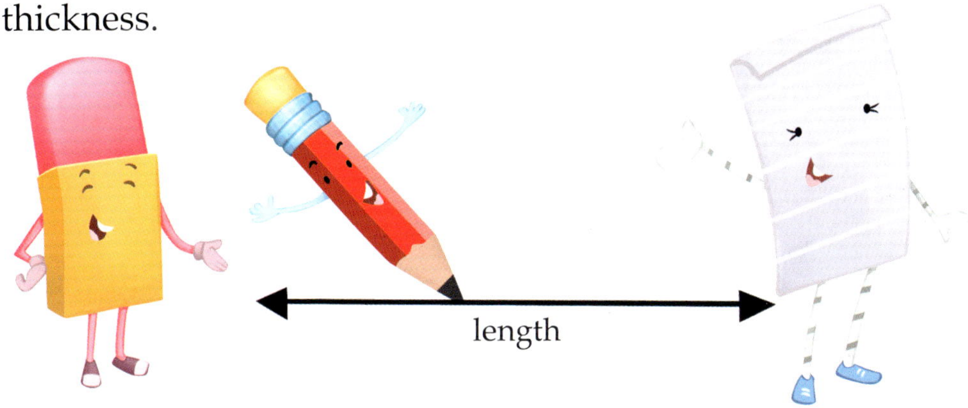

When you have two dimensions, it means you can go forward and backward in a line and also turn in a new direction to start another line. The lines in a rectangle move in two directions. In a circle, you continuously turn in new directions as you draw.

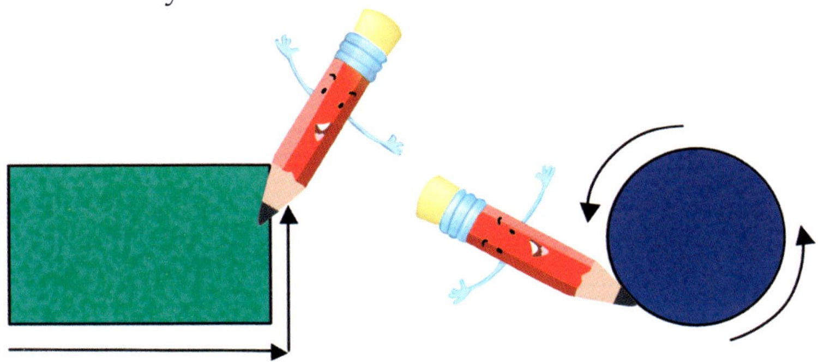

POCKET FACT

A point is zero-dimensional. It has neither length nor breadth.

A Polygon hunt

A polygon is a flat, 2-D plane shape with only straight lines. A polygon can have any number of sides.

Quiz

Which of these are polygons?

Hint: A polygon is a shape with all straight lines.

Answer:

Polygons and Angles

In some polygons, the sides meet in a square corner. This is called a **right angle**.

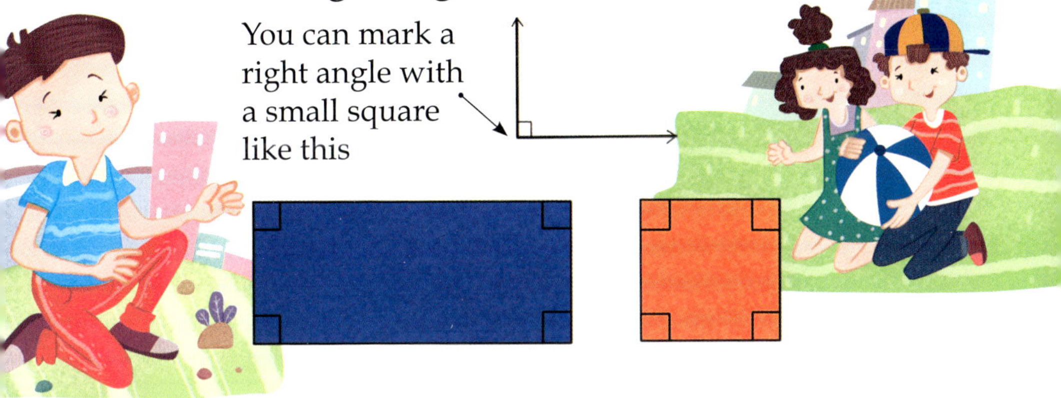

The four sides in a rectangle and a square always meet at right angles.

Not all polygons have sides that meet at right angles. Sometimes the corners are wider or narrower than a right angle.

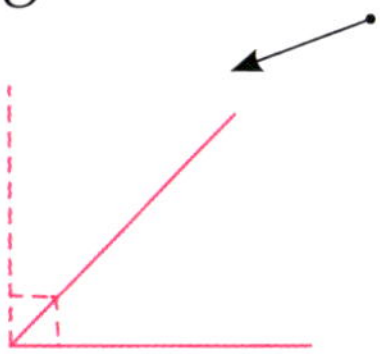

An **acute angle** is a corner that is smaller or narrower than a right angle.

An **obtuse angle** is a corner that is greater or wider than a right angle.

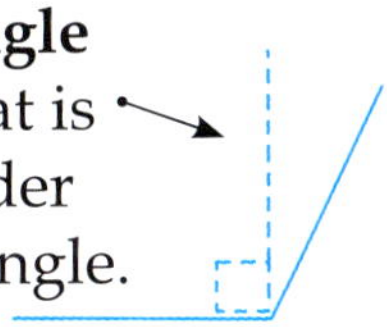

You can draw a curve to mark these angles

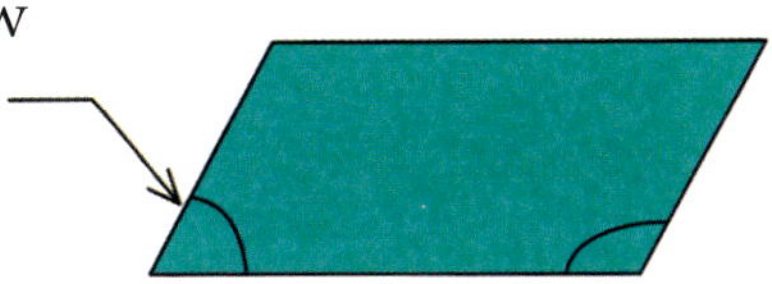

Perpendicular lines

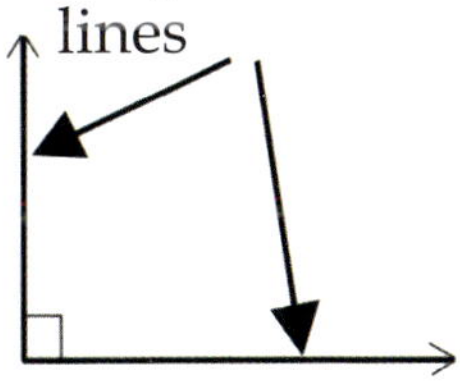

DID YOU KNOW?

Perpendicular lines are lines that meet at right angles.

Quadrilaterals

All four-sided polygons are called **Quadrilaterals**.

A parallelogram is a quadrilateral where the opposite sides are equal. A rectangle is a parallelogram with sides that meet at right angles.

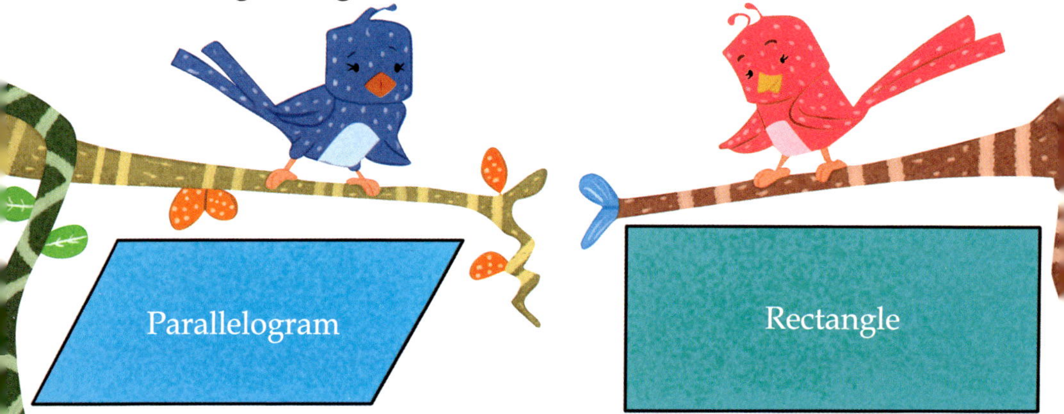

A **Rhombus** is a quadrilateral where all four sides are equal. When the sides of a rhombus meet at right angles, we call it a square. A square is a rhombus, but not all rhombuses are squares.

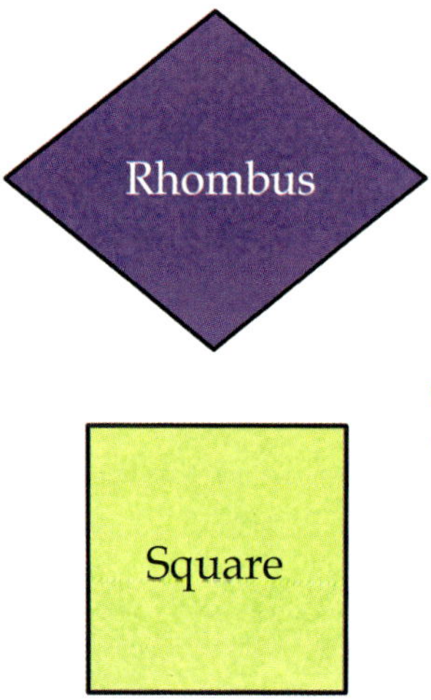

POCKET FACT

A square is a special type of a rectangle. A square is a rhombus too.

Quadrilateral Family Tree

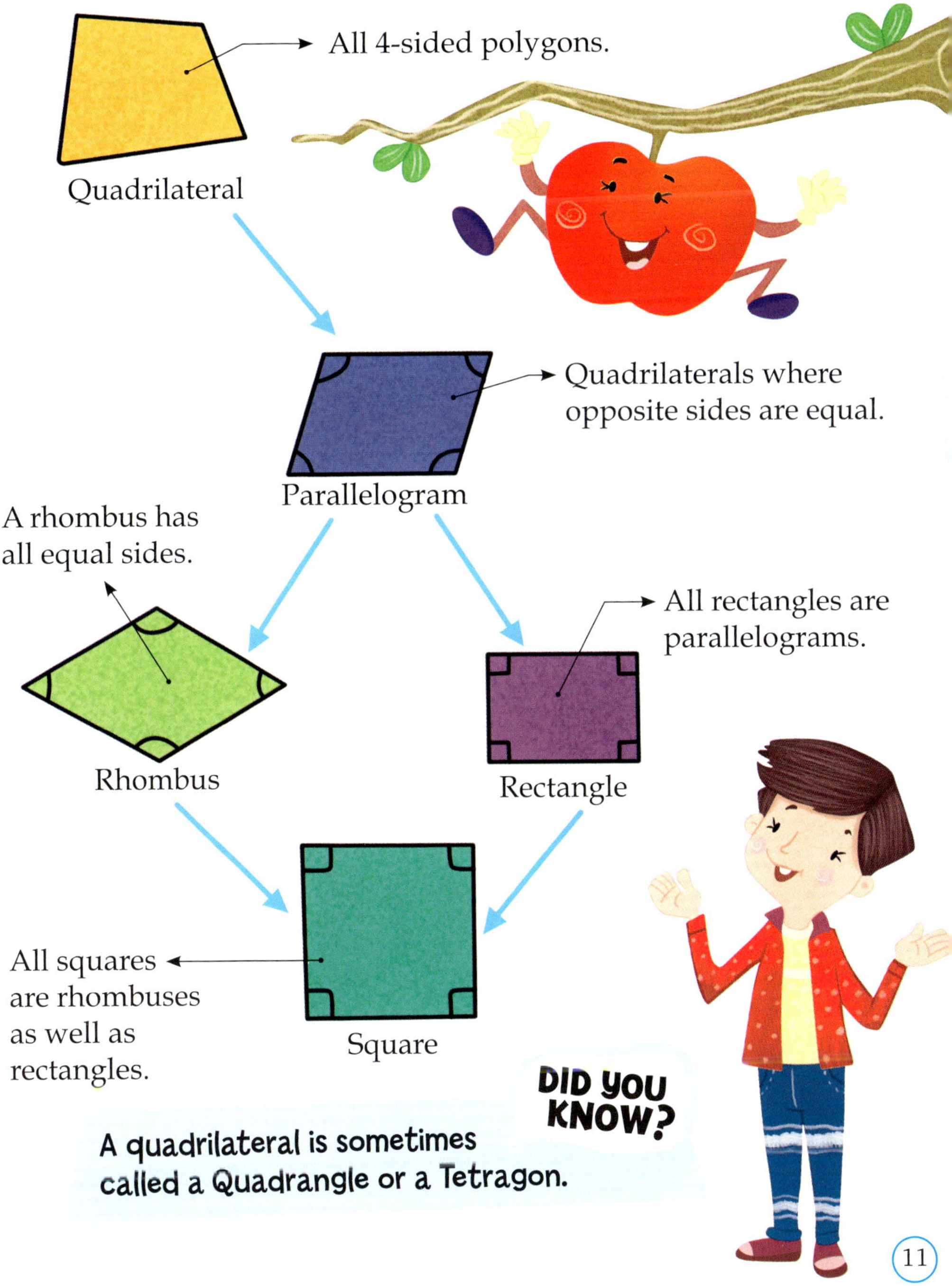

DID YOU KNOW?

A quadrilateral is sometimes called a Quadrangle or a Tetragon.

Sorting Triangles

A **triangle** is a three-sided polygon. Three special names have been given to triangles that tell how many sides are of equal lengths.

An **equilateral triangle** has all equal sides. Take three matchsticks and put them together like a triangle. All matchsticks are of equal length. You just made an equilateral triangle.

An **isosceles triangle** has two equal sides.

Break one of the matchsticks such that it is shorter than the other two. Put them together in a triangle again. This time only two sides are of equal length. This is an isosceles triangle.

A **scalene triangle** has no equal sides.

Break another matchstick such that none of the matchsticks are of equal length. You can still put them together into a triangle. None of the sides of this scalene triangle are the same length.

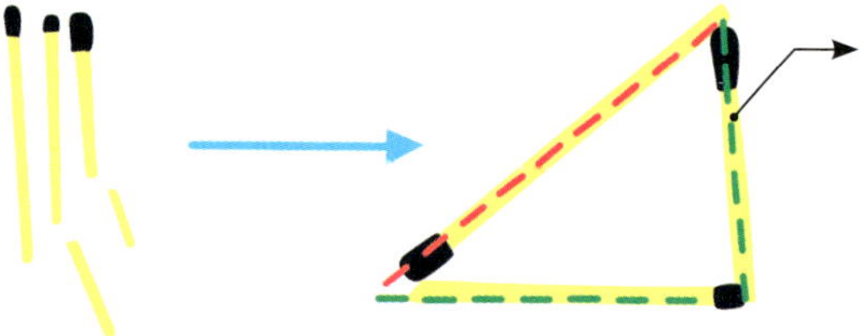

These three special names tell what kind of angles the triangle has.

A **right triangle** has a right angle in one of its corners.

An **acute triangle** has all angles narrower than a right angle (acute angle).

An **obtuse triangle** has one angle wider than a right angle (obtuse angle).

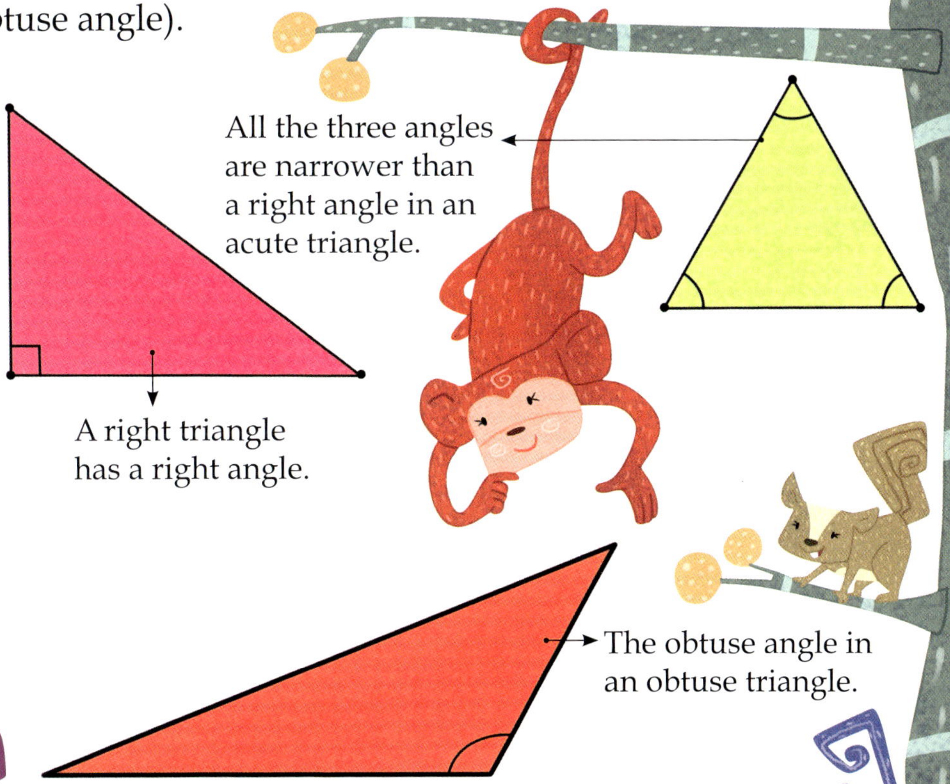

Quiz

If a Right Isosceles triangle has a right angle and two equal sides, what is an Obtuse Scalene triangle?

Answer: A triangle with an obtuse angle and no equal sides.

3. Activity: Terrific Tangrams

Tangrams are fun puzzles made of seven plane(2-D) shapes.

A tangram is a Chinese puzzle that is made by cutting a square into seven pieces

You can use the pieces to make different patterns as shown below. Remember, you have to use all seven pieces for your pattern and the pieces cannot overlap.

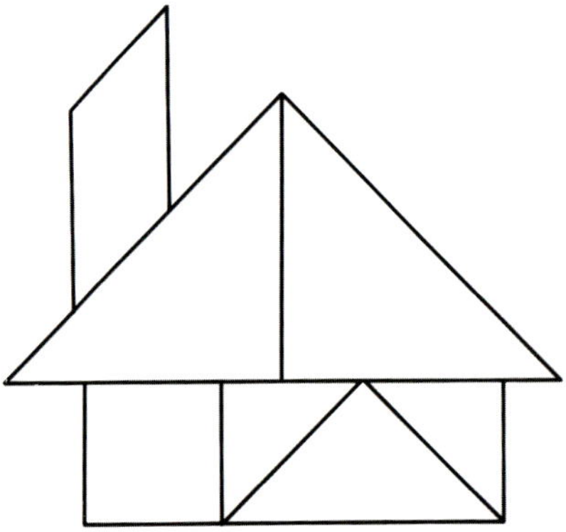

A house

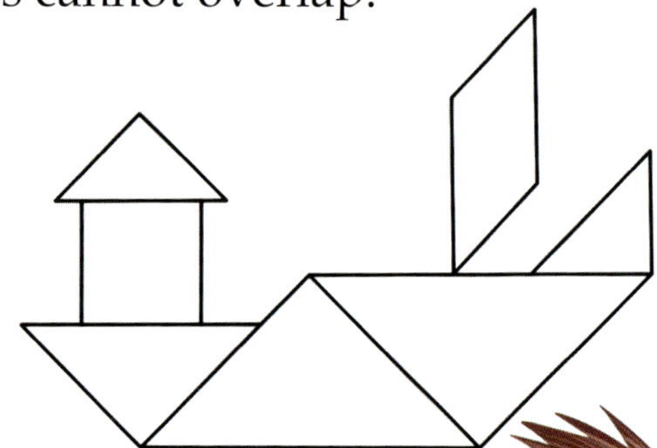

A ship

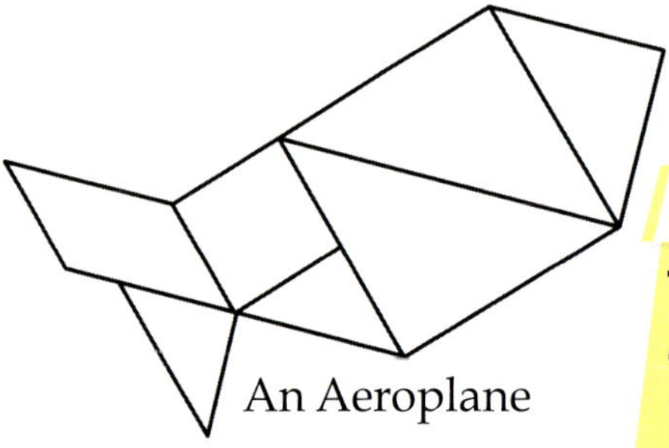

An Aeroplane

POCKET FACT

Tangrams are used to create different patterns including animals, people, numbers, geometric shapes and much more.

Create your own Tangram puzzle

You need:

- A plain white, square sheet of paper
- Pencil
- Colour pencils or crayons
- Scissors, ruler

Step 1. Make a square grid on your sheet of paper. For this, fold the sheet in half, then again fold further in half. Repeat along the other side. Draw lightly along the fold lines.

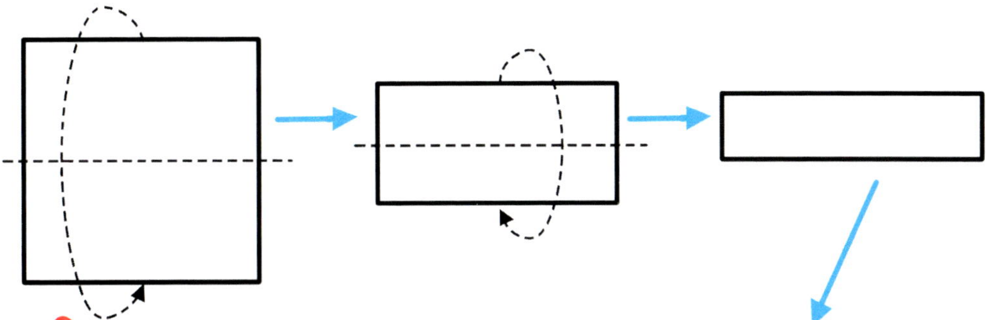

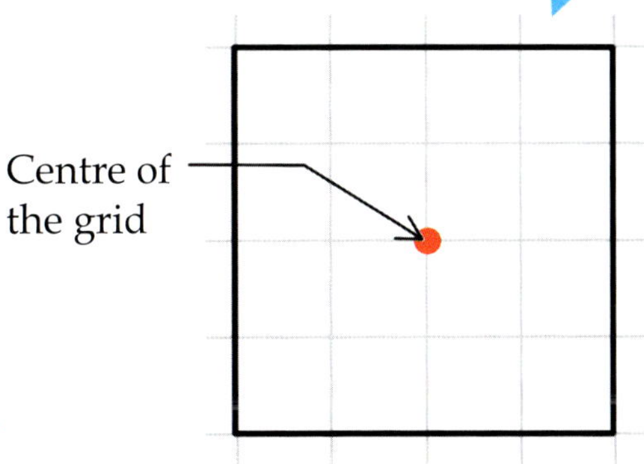

Step 2. Draw out lines that will mark the sides of each tangram piece as shown, using the grid lines as a guide.

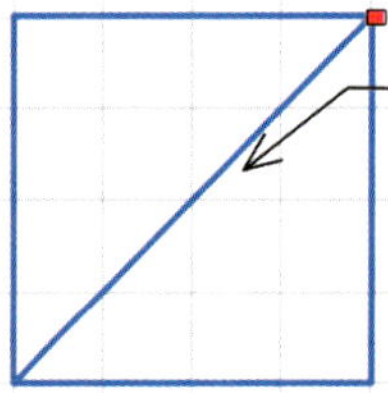

1. Join the opposite corners.

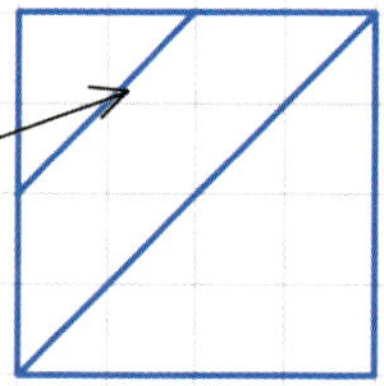

2. Create another triangle in the top left corner.

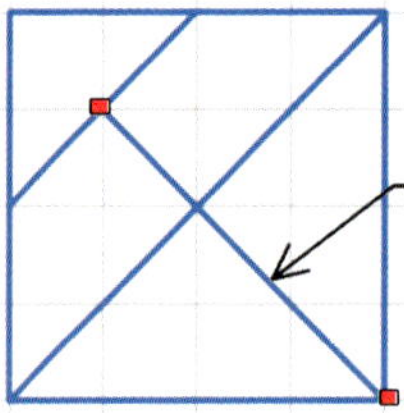

3. Join the bottom corner to the centre of the grid and stop at the second line.

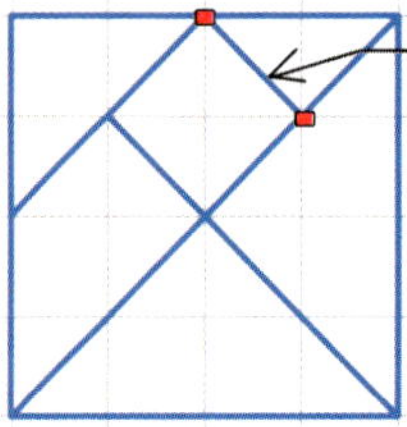

4. Draw a line to join the first and second lines.

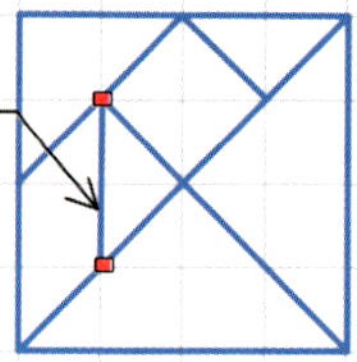

5. Draw your last line from where your second line meets the third line. End at the first line.

Step 3. Fill the puzzle pieces with different colours and cut along the lines. Your tangram puzzle is ready.

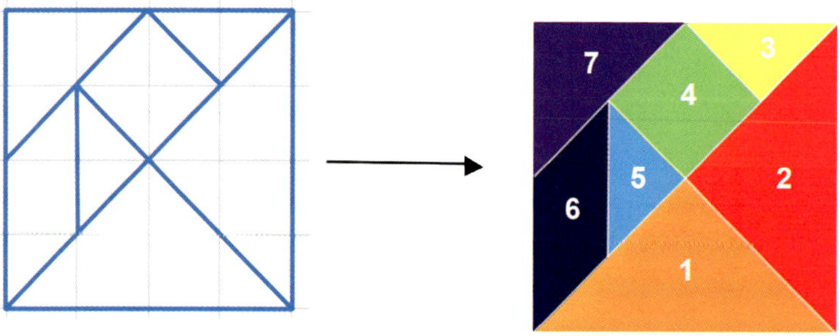

Step 4. Make these interesting patterns using your tangram puzzle pieces.

Cat

Tree

House

Rocket

POCKET FACT

The tangram puzzle pieces are called tans.

4. Solid Shapes

Look at this dice. What do you think this dice has that the square beside it does not have?

The dice has thickness.

This square is a plane shape with no thickness.

Like the dice, most objects we see around us are solid shapes. Solid or 3-D shapes have three measurements – length, breadth and height. These together form the three dimensions of a 3-D shape.

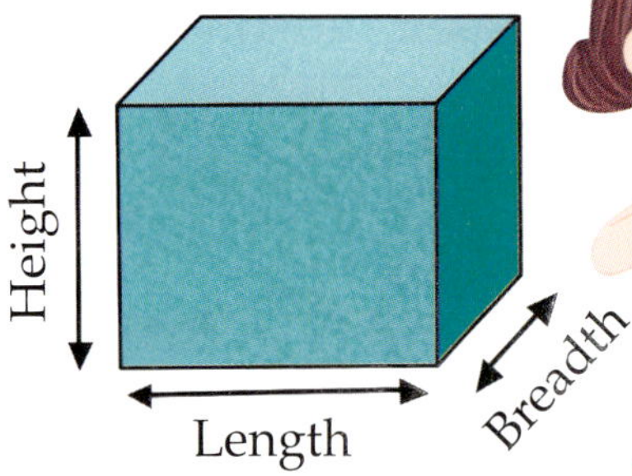

A 3-D shape with three dimensions.

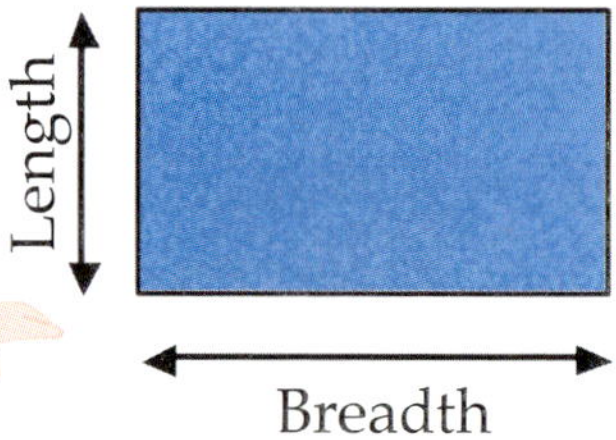

A 2-D shape with two dimensions.

POCKET FACT

In the world of 3-D, you can move forward, backward, sideways as well as up and down.

Faces, Edges and Vertices

A 3-D shape has faces, edges and vertices. Do you know where they are?

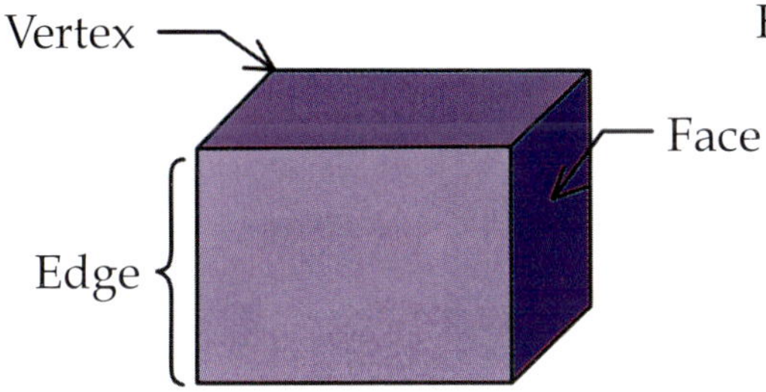

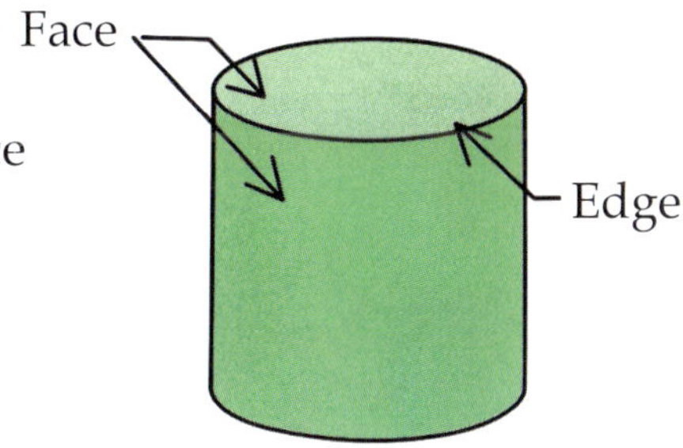

A **face** is the flat or curved surface on a 3-D shape.

An **edge** is the line where two faces meet.

A **vertex** is the corner where two or more edges meet.

Faces, edges and vertices are attributes or properties of a 3-D shape. Different shapes have different numbers of faces, edges and vertices. All shapes have faces. In a 2-D shape, the face is the flat part of the shape.

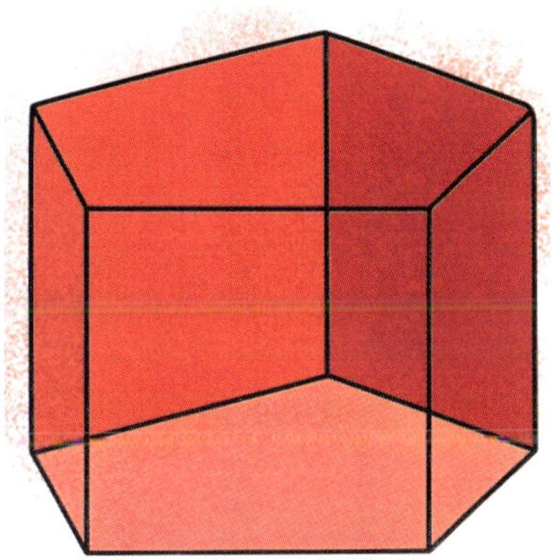

DID YOU KNOW?

Vertices is the plural form for Vertex.

What's the Shape?

Cubes and **Cuboids** are shaped like boxes.
They both have

- 6 Flat Faces
- 8 Vertices
- 12 Edges

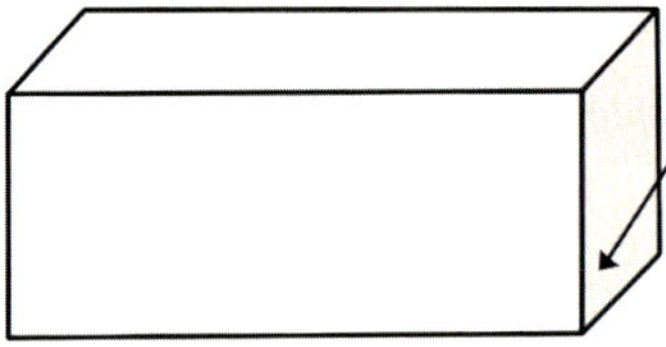

All the angles in **cubes** and **cuboids** are right angles.

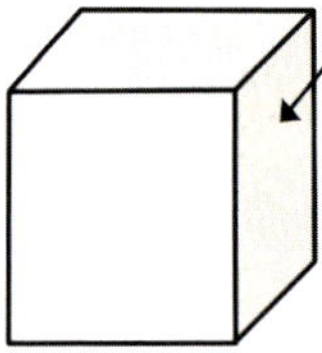

In a cube all sides have the same length.

length = breadth = height

Quiz

Charlie had to collect only cube-shaped objects for a class project. But he mixed up cubes with cuboids. Can you pick out the cube-shaped objects for him?

Answer:

A **sphere** is round like a ball. It has one face, zero vertices and zero edges.

A **sphere** only has a curved face.

The beads in this pearl necklace are spheres.

You can find a sphere in a basketball.

A sphere decoration ball.

Bubbles are perfect spheres.

DID YOU KNOW?

The Sun, moon and the Earth are all spheres.

A **cone** is a 3-D shape that narrows smoothly from a flat circular base to a point. A cone has:

- 1 curved face
- 1 or 0 circular flat face
- 1 vertex
- 1 curved edge

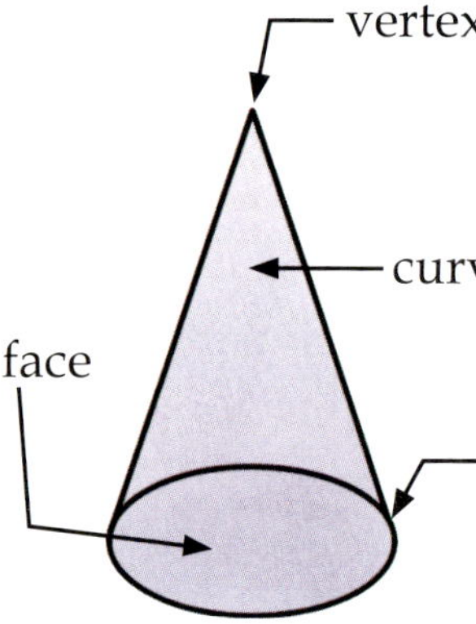

Traffic cones you sometimes see on the road.

One of your favourite cone -an ice cream cone.

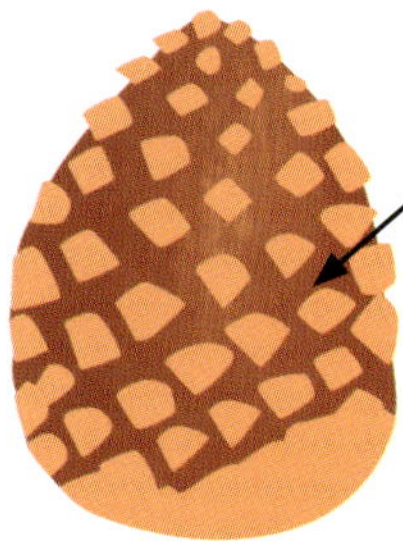

A pine cone is called so because of its conical shape.

We love wearing cone-shaped party hats.

POCKET FACT

The vertex of a cone is also called an apex.

A cylinder is shaped like a can. It contains two flat, circular bases connected by a curved surface. A cylinder has:

- 1 curved face
- 0, 1 or 2 circular flat faces at both ends
- 0 vertices
- 2 curved edges

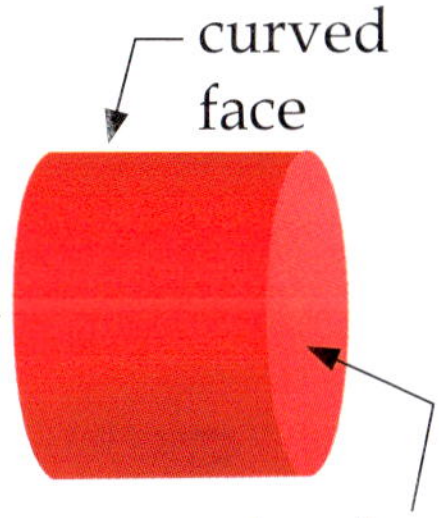

Cylindrical soda cans

A drinking straw is a cylinder with zero flat faces.

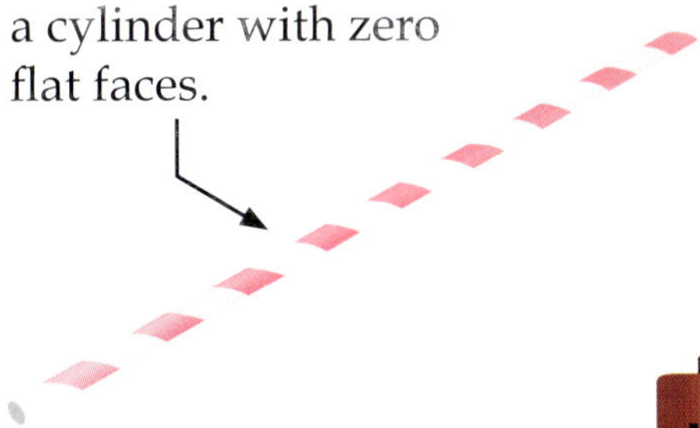

Battery cells are often cylindrical in shape.

Many candles are cylinders to start with, but melt into a pool of wax when they burn.

Quiz

Can you think of another cylindrical object that has no flat faces?

Answer: A pipe or a hose is open at both ends. It has no flat face, only a curved surface.

Stack, Slide Or Roll?

Felix is trying to place these items on top of each other. Which shapes will stack?

The marbles **(spheres)** will not stack over each other as they are curvy.

The flat faces help these boxes (**cubes and cuboids**) easily stack up.

But, you cannot stack these carrots (**cone**) this way.

You cannot stack them like this either.

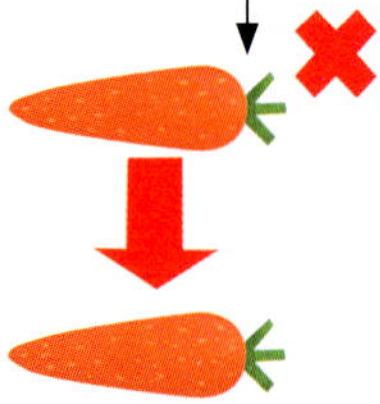

You can stack these cones only because the pointed top of one cone fits into the hollow part of another cone.

These logs (**cylinders**) will not stack on top of each other over their curved surface.

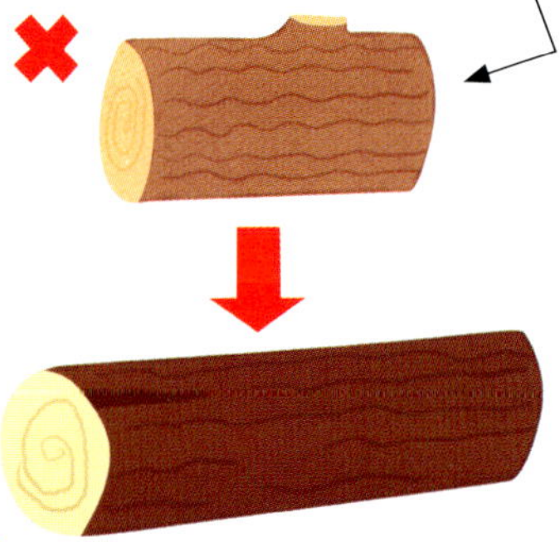

These boxes (**cylinders**) will stack up on their flat surfaces.

POCKET FACT

Shapes need a flat surface to stack and slide. They cannot stack or slide on their curved surfaces.

Felix is pushing the shapes down a slope. Which shapes will slide?

To slide, a shape needs a flat face. Cubes and cuboids slide easily. A sphere will not slide as it has no flat face. A cylinder slides only on its flat ends. A cone too, slides only on its flat end.

Felix is pushing the shapes once again down a slope. Which shapes will roll?

To roll, a shape needs a curvy surface. Cubes and cuboids do not roll as they have no curved surface. A sphere will roll as it is curvy all around. A cylinder rolls only on its curved side. A cone, rolls to one side on its curved surface as it has a pointed top (apex).

3-D Shape Investigations

Felix recorded all his observations at one place on this chart.

Shape	Does it Roll?	Does it Slide?	Does it Stack?
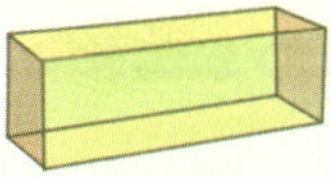 Cuboid	No. It has only flat faces.	Yes, as it has all flat faces	Yes, as it has all flat faces.
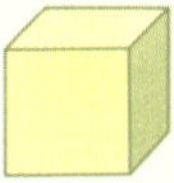 Cube	No. It has only flat faces.	Yes, as it has all flat faces.	Yes, as it has all flat faces.
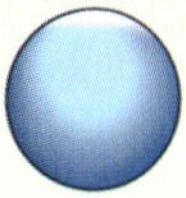 Sphere	Yes. It is curved all around.	No, because it has no flat face.	No, because it rolls over on its curvy surface.
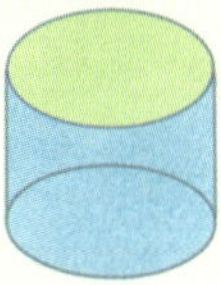 Cylinder	Yes, but only on its curved surface.	Yes, but only on its flat ends.	Yes, but only on its flat ends, not on its curved surface.
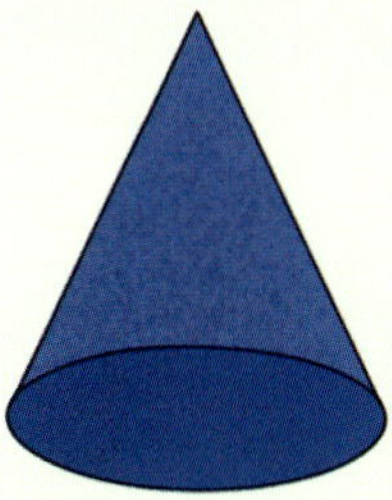 Cone	Yes, but it rolls to one side around its vertex.	Yes, but only on its flat base.	Yes, a cone can stack on another shape on its flat base. No, another shape cannot stack on a cone as it has a point on the top.

Let's Get Active

Choose the correct option

1. A 3-D shape that rolls.

   (a) Cone (b) Cube

   (c) Square (d) Circle

2. I am a 2-D shape. I am round. I have 0 corners.

   (a) Rectangle (b) Triangle

   (c) Square (d) Circle

3. I am a 3-D shape. I roll and I slide. I have 1 circular flat surface.

   (a) Cube (b) Cone

   (c) Sphere (d) Cylinder

4. Stack these shapes:

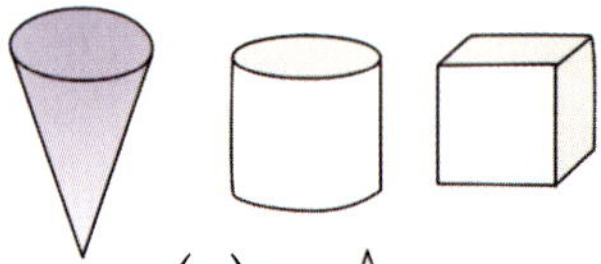

(a) 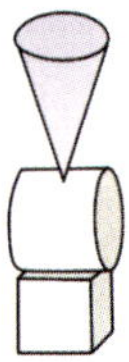 (b) 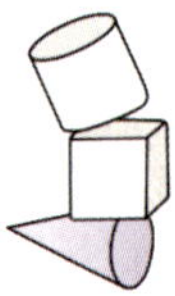 (c) 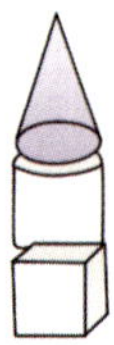

5. Count the number of triangles:

   (a) 1 (b) 3

   (c) 4 (d) 5

Know your shapes

State whether the following statements are true or false.

1. An isosceles triangle has two equal sides. (True/False)
2. A right angle makes a square corner. (True/False)
3. 2-D shapes have thickness. (True/False)
4. 3-D shapes are solid shapes. (True/False)
5. All rhombuses are squares. (True/False)
6. Circles and ellipses are polygons. (True/False)

Find the shapes

Find and count the shapes you see in the picture.

Circles		Square	
Triangles		Rectangles	
Cones		Cubes/Cuboids	
Spheres		Cylinders	

Solve the Problems

1	Emily's family is building a swimming pool in the shape of a hexagon. How many sides will the pool have?	
2	Kaleb learnt that this shape has 6 flat faces, 8 vertices and 12 edges of the same length. What shape did he learn about?	
3	How many flat faces does the moon have?	
4	While drawing on some scrap paper, Jerry drew a shape with three equal sides. What shape did he draw?	
5	Sarah was investigating a 3-D shape that had three faces. She learnt that she could stack and slide the shape on its two faces, but not on the third. She could roll the object on one face but not on the other two. What is the name of the 3-D shape?	

GLOSSARY

Backward	directed behind or to the rear
Breadth	the distance or measurement from side to side of something; width
Curved	bent
Dimension	a measurable extent of a particular kind, such as length, breadth, depth, or height
Flat	having a level surface
Forward	towards the front
Geometry	a branch of mathematics
Height	the measurement of something from base to top
Length	the measurement or extent of something from end to end
Narrower	to be smaller
Opposite	situated on the other or further side
Pattern	an arrangement or design
Puzzle	a game, toy, or problem
Sideways	towards, or from the side
Straight	without a curve or bend.
Wider	to be greater or more in size

ANSWERS

Page 28. 1(a) 2(d) 3(b)
4(c) 5(d)

Page 29. (1) True (2) True
(3) False (4) True
(5) False (6) False

Page 31. (1) 6 (2) cube
(3) zero (4) equilateral triangle
(5) cylinder